The Mystery Still Drives Us

J.K. McDowell

Foreword by Amy Nawrocki

WAYFARER
BOOKS

WAYFARER
BOOKS

Quantity sales. Special discounts are available on quantity purchases by corporations, associations, bookstores, and others. For details, contact the publisher or visit wholesalers such as Ingram or Baker & Taylor.

All Rights Reserved
Published in 2021 by Wayfarer Books
Cover Image: © David Billings
Back Cover Pattern: Vector geometric pattern from Alhambra Granada, Spain
Cover Design and Interior Design by Jason Kirkey & Leslie M. Browning
PAPERBACK ISBN: 978-1-953340-10-8
EBOOK ISBN: 978-1-953340-11-5
First Edition Trade Paperback

10 9 8 7 6 5 4 3 2 1

Wayfarer Books, is committed to ecological stewardship. We greatly value the natural environment and invest in environmental conservation. For each book purchased in our online store we plant one tree.

CONTENTS

xi   Foreword by Amy Nawrocki

3   …a different poem.

4   …a scratch.

5   …almost lost.

6   …always dreaming.

7   …always here.

8   …always hold.

9   …always Love more.

10   …always stranger.

11   …and human.

12   …and truths confused.

13   …and waiting.

14   …any creative life.

15   …are unfinished.

16   …be unimaginable.

17   …beginning comes.

18   …beyond the worst.

19   …brought you here.

20   …Carcosa returns.

21   …come together.

22   …compel us.

23   …could escape.

24   …dream form.

25   …every touch.

26   …everything.

27   …few endure.

28   ...focus there.

29   ...forever lost.

30   ...future awaits.

31   ...heal us.

32   ...hidden doorways.

33   ...in sorrows.

34   ...into place.

35   ...is your poetry.

36   ...just float.

37   ...linger.

38   ...meet you there.

39   ...more recollection.

40   ...move forward.

41   ...my light.

42   ...my name.

43   ...my sanctuary.

44   ...my steps.

45   ...my terrors.

46   ...my things.

47   ...never miss.

48   ...no hazard.

49   ...Not at an End.

50   ...not that poem.

51   ...nothing else.

52   ...of endarkenment.

53   ...of living.

54   ...of sovereignty.

55   ...open seas.

56   ...or night.

57   ...sea chantey.

58   ...so drink.

59   ...something else entirely.

60   …Tell me.

61   …the challenge.

62   …the hanging tree.

63   …the mirrors.

64   …the modern.

65   …the next frost.

66   …the stabbing.

67   …these days?

68   …to give.

69   …to justice.

70   …together.

71   …too well.

72   …uncanny shadows.

73   …was lonely.

74   …wild patience.

75   …with honey.

76   …yes and go.

77   …yes, silence.

78   …your art.

79   …your eyes.

80   …your poetry.

FOREWORD
by Amy Nawrocki

QUESTION: IS A POEM A CONTAINER OR CONTENTS? It's a good query, one that a poem provokes inherently. J.K. McDowell likes such questions, and he ponders them diligently. The answer depends. Do you conjure a milk carton holding the face of a lost child? Or feel the existential weight of a jar precariously placed high on a hill in Tennessee? A poem is both an *idea* and a *thing*. For McDowell, this is a central paradox, and for his readers, an invitation. In his latest collection, he confirms both that "the mystery still drives us" and that answers are possible.

McDowell tackles the question of poem-as-container through a modified ghazal form. Typically structured in two-line couplets, ghazal stanzas are structured as syntactically self-contained units, usually end-stopped, creating a ladder for the reader to climb. Each poem is held together by theme, emotion, and language as well as other formal elements like rhyme and repetition. In McDowell's adaptation, he uses a three-lime stanza, and each poem has six stanzas. We could say his container is a little bigger, the scope of the idea a little broader, sturdier. Each title provokes us with an ellipse; the last line brings us back, repeating the phrase, building "an everlasting chain." And we need a strong container, for the contents are volatile.

McDowell's voice is deeply personal, clearly linked to the inner mind of the writer. "My critical eye is blind to what I need to be shown." At the same time, the ghazal tradition is to incorporate the poet's name in each poem, so the poet creates another persona, one who speaks directly to a metaphorical J.K., sometimes in the familiar calling him "Jim," sometimes more formally: "Step carefully James, Beauty is underfoot in / all directions." This voice can quell fears, hold the lamp through dark paths, incite caution, and even chastise. The poet, therefore, is the speaker *and* the listener. This accomplishment is both the *how* and the *why* of the collection. Both voices carry us from page to page, the dialogue sounding a lot like what we hear in our own heads whenever we get trapped in the echo of vulnerability.

What should a poem contain? Water and sand, scorpions and soft cotton, "whiskey notes and traded promises"? Throughout his tiered strophes, "the polished shield becomes the polished mirror." McDowell leads us to the cliff's edge and exposes what is universally felt: deep fears and exasperated longings; the pain of loss and the search for truth. What is sacred? How far away is the past? How daunting is the future without some thread to carry us forward? Where can the soul find nourishment; from what and from whom? Is poetry enough?

> There is a turning that orbits the truth. Not the
> Spin that offers a lens of distortion. Rather
> A bearing that honors the many centers, here and there.

It is easy to lose our way. The container is heavy; the contents can be elusive. Nevertheless, we hold on. We lift ourselves a little higher. As McDowell learns, "Never forget the sacred words that brought you here."

J.K. McDowell is generous enough to make his inner consciousness audible and to give us a container that fits a weary soul. What's held inside is nourishing and familiar. Questions are answered with more questions because the mystery still drives us. "Tell me James K., these poems, are they sketches /Of the soul—shadows, signposts, silhouettes?" Read on. They contain all.

...a different poem.

The horrors "From Beyond" are never easy to face.
Temptations and terrors bleed into each other
And will not blend. Separate but equal never works.

The Dance, what Mystery! This is the seeing that
Makes the eyes bleed. Eternities evaporate
As you slice the skin from the well-practiced floor craft.

The absinthe paints an "Unnamable" seduction.
As the 13th hour approaches, I witness
The betwixt and between bleed through the veil.

Wounds bleed sap and the rot spreads. We both know my friend
You would not survive the next storm. A lily grows
Where you used to stand. The axes had to come.

The remedy, exsanguination—the Darkness!
The rubies of the Soul bleed across the cursed forest floor.
They are my guide and sustenance as I seek You.

From Beyond? Jim, tell me about the horrors
From Within. Fears bleed underneath the attraction.
Sorry, I forgot, that is a different poem.

...a scratch.

A blank page, the clean canvas, that patient slab of stone.
Accept or decline. Neither completes their existence,
Nor yours—oh by the way, you never start from scratch.

The glass fills too many times. Manners float away.
Our patience runs thin, just before the blood spills
He is saved, there is the irritation to scratch.

The bad days, best to ignore them. There are the
Good days that spill with inspiration. The downside
Is too often I cannot decipher my own scratch.

There are mixed emotions and obscure references.
Honestly, I am not enjoying your tears.
Thankfully, at least the writing is up to scratch.

Lie still Jim! There is no chase, no destination.
The flares light the night sky. Please, you must believe me
Jim, these lacerations are more than just a scratch.

We lay out our fears like poker cards at the call.
Eagle, or crow, or macaw it does not matter.
The touch of the holy claw always leaves a scratch.

...almost lost.

You were too well lit for the others to notice,
But I could not miss this singular gift of presence,
The shade of your fluttering heart, my sweet precious.

A patchwork of unfinished phrasings,
Fragmented feelings and forgotten meanings.
The frustration and fatigue of this moonlight poetry.

I am lucky, though often obsessed by waking
Nightmares. At times I have seen the crows of
Memory gather in threats but never in murders.

Serious snacks: Black olives, pitted, sumptuous.
Sharp cheddar with chive, splendidly sliced.
Sips of whiskey and serious consequences.

Graphite curves, smooth with sharp endings. Sketches and
Studies, lifetimes of finished and unfinished works.
Jim, trace the depth of form, not reflective surfaces.

There are dreams, soft whispers that move between souls,
Not belonging to any one voice, reciting oaths
Of ancient alliances and friendships almost lost.

...*always dreaming.*

See there, in The Greatest Two Minutes in Sports,
The moment of the turn and the race decided.
Mud splatter, hoof beats, the winner—Always Dreaming.

A collision evasion algorithm trained on mirages.
Technology's truth does not serve your selfishness.
Avoid the crash? My friend you must be dreaming.

There is no escape from the thin fingers of Death.
Dying shadows shift in a Detroit hotel room.
The cards were played and the Darkness was caught dreaming.

Did you read about asphyxiated aspirations?
These crimes continue, rarely lead to death.
Lack of oxygen does keep people from dreaming.

I am caught betwixt nevermore and eternal recurring.
My shattered face in the midnight mirror has
"The seeming of a demon that is dreaming."

Few things are more dangerous than a Jinn hiding
In a flaming desert whirlwind. I know James, eyes
Open or eyes closed, you are always dreaming.

...always here.

Hear the song. The music is all around us,
All the time. Too often our worlds become smears
Of colored sand. Look closely, we are all here.

Hear the call. Your Heart is speaking to you.
Shiny distractions and whitewash indifference
Do not last. If you're not listening, why are you here?

Hear the screams. Wounds to the Soul scar over, as throats
Are scraped raw by cruel gestures and crueler intensions.
Fingerprints of torture remain, no one is here.

Hear the whispers. Trace the shapes of lips and other
Soft places that lovers know. These imaginings
Will help you remember the dreams that brought you here.

Hear the distant thunder, storms approach despite
The sunshine. At best the forecast is only good for
A few hours. Despite the weather, she is not here.

Hear my heart beat out of rhythm. I sympathize
James. The spirals' touch informs and interferes. This
Is reality, the spirits are always here.

...*always hold.*

Anise and fennel blooms toward a lucid dreaming.
The equations are written clearly—still the
Solution is obscured. Something is missing.

Another calendar year tramples over
Shattered dreams. Why do you collect the shards
Instead of going back to the clay and the wheel?

Desert flowers answer the call of the nighttime sky.
The cliff face glyphs catch the flicker of the fire.
Poetry chases the sparks and cinders star-ward.

Leylines? I am looking for the Spiral within.
That churning energy that spins you, pulls in tight
And sweeps outward over the Soul's hidden landscape.

Please, the thoughts today have been needlessly sharp.
My eyes close, tired of points and counterpoints.
This change in vision brings us no closer to home.

An undated love letter from more than a
Decade ago. Today the same devotion,
Unshaken—lives challenged Jim, but those ties always hold.

… always Love more.

There is much to celebrate and much to lament.
The alchemy works! Too long I have used
Detachment as a shield against enchantment. No more!

Bible or no, "Fisher of Men," we all know the phrase.
Caught in the Net, the Matrix, the Mesh… Sorting the
Digital debris of "Likes," we always want more.

Auto-drive is stuck on Accelerationist.
We want, we want, we want. Really? A cancerous
Ecology confuses abundance with more.

Morning breaks, the cardinal calls, the conure screeches.
Two empty shells, lives found shattered. Not a good day.
Jesus they are not listening anymore.

A parabolic path over rusted razor
Wire, the flaming arrow strikes me center chest,
Only to find my Heart is missing. Please feel more.

These Shadows, uninvited guests, arrive late.
Still, torture, murder and genocide are not welcome.
Never forget James, you can always Love more.

...*always stranger.*

We cross into the season of named storms.
This dreaming dust awaits a baptism by lightning.
Realize that a once familiar shore is now stranger.

A flash of insight is often needed to move
Along the spirals of memory and belonging.
Odds are the face in the mirror is stranger.

A darkness fills wonderland and the hookah burns
With a new blend of herbs. Inhales, curiousier
And curiousier, become even stranger.

Strength and honor, we stand in the danger beyond
The pale. Weaponless at the ready, hands clasped,
"So say we all" in a cadence never stranger.

The steel for vermin. Despite your justified
Atrocities James, the beheading by a friend is
Always preferred to any cut by a stranger.

Duende, so close to death, this poetic pursuit.
There is no choice here, the inexplicable fears
Disappear and what remains is always stranger.

...and human.

In letters, Vallejo sent me his Decembers.
No return postage, I kept his Januarys too.
Evidence for my defense? Gravely, I say yes.

The tools, simple: a maul, spikes and rough-hewn timbers.
The hours: dawn to dusk. The pay: very meager.
The clients: criminals—oh and that other fellow.

She knew how to pay attention. The Unexpected
Silence of her eyes, the tedious inspection.
Please turn off the light, fingertips are better.

On the longest night, I gaze at a single
Candle flame. Clouds hide the night sky and I am safe.
My dreams and my terrors before dawn have much to teach.

The season of named storms comes to a close.
The plywood comes down from the second floor windows.
Light fills the upstairs dark, the ghosts bask in sunlight.

Eyes colored eternity, skin cold granite smooth.
Your tears of grief roll off their feathered wings.
I can offer a warm embrace, frail and human.

…and truths confused.

I have eaten my imagination by mistake.
Healer, tell me how does soul mending work?
This is a wounding before "once upon a time."

Leap but do not expect the net to appear.
That extra day last month set you back weeks.
An apocalypse planner is rarely reliable.

I suppose the anger is from a zigzag mix
Of emptiness and enchantment. Freezer burn,
These leftovers, even warmed, are unfit to eat.

Tonight the call goes out cryptically universal.
Touching everyone and impacting a few.
Spirit fingers tipped with invisible sparklers.

Mealtime, the woodpecker hammers the oak, a distant
Yet reassuring sound. Hallowed echoes and
Elsewhere dinner conversation dissolves in anguish.

James, this is an asymmetrical voyeurism.
Infection and conjuring, touched at a distance.
Dances of windows, mirrors and truths confused.

…and waiting.

What do you hope to learn during this interview?
Will you record and report truthfully,
All, even of your failures? Are you ready to begin?

Sometimes there are no words for your joy and no words
For my sorrow. I am the pillow trapped between
Othello and Desdemona—no wonder I can't sleep.

I know you, Son of a Dark Stranger. Do not
Deny that you are a student of The Moor.
Calligraphy, alchemy and the blade, expose your ways.

Begin at the Jamaa el Fna. A headless spirit
Will lead you through the maze of the Marrakesh souks.
Find me, I am waiting under the Yellow Sign.

"Fulfillment." "Closure." These headlines sell advertising.
This puzzle is your design, ever-changing and eternal.
No solution, only the ever-engaging play. Never stop.

James you wander the empty; modern and ancient.
A walk-about abandoned, unsustainable creative sprints,
Dismissed as insubstantial, yet real and hungry and waiting.

. . . any creative life.

A fresh corpse hangs in the branches and I know
I am now in the right part of the jungle forest.
The question is my Friend, where is the Jaguar?

What blight and oblivion feed his intellect?
What neglect and disregard feed her revenge?
Blades crisscross—know these are not two separate questions.

The air is thin, the spaces between are even
Thinner. Do not panic, a soft breath sometimes
Stays unnoticed by the terrors. I did say sometimes.

I turn my face away in perfect timing
As the multitude of boils on my right arm
Burst in fluidic fireworks. This is a good dream.

The engravings on this ancient skull are not
Postmortem. I wonder at the fine skill and
Psychotropics, the courage of both healer and healed.

James, I just finished reading your obituary out loud.
The portraits on the wrinkled bills in my wallet wept in grief.
No currency can lengthen the thread of any creative life.

...are unfinished.

I know those cane fields, the solitary oak
Thick with years of suffering that defy the
Even spaced rows of cultivated intentions.

She was curved and sharp and not unprepared.
The blade, Damascus steel; the sheath, Meknes artistry.
My eyes and my tongue, careful in their tracing.

He never liked the sound—that clink of ice in
A glass of whiskey. Chilling reminders of
Watered-down spirits and failed hauntings.

Passions of the flesh, intimate escapes in
Closeness, desperate to resist this flat existence.
No more hording of doubt, Death is Love's trump card.

What is inspired James K.? Painting in darkness,
Your self-portrait of shadow, without a mirror.
Too many times Friend, these works are unfinished.

...be unimaginable.

There are gliding curves that remind me of your kindness.
The crossings are meaningful, serene collisions.
Scarlet scribblings fade in the tears of blank spaces.

At times in a softly shaded red-gold brilliance,
Blended souls lie indistinct in the thin grass
Under the great and low arms of this massive oak.

In these moments of profound joy step out of
Beingness into the thin places between worlds.
Membranes of pure music sustaining silent doorways.

We are lost across lifetimes striving in perfect
Failure to realize that so much is in our grasp
If we just open our hearts and share our gifts.

We know cleverness can take you only so far.
Of course death reminds us that love is eternal.
Awe and bewilderment are written on our bones.

Every moment James, you can stir the spirit to find
A new vantage point and discover a vista
That would otherwise be unimaginable.

...beginning comes.

They must have always been there, the rotting breath,
The cruel stares, the festering and foul whispers.
Yet, I never ask myself, "Who are these people?"

Choose: the eye of the needle; the head of a pin.
Angels and camels, counting and recounting,
And despite the outcome, we miss the point.

We need to keep reminding each other of
The uncountable connections to the beautiful
And the numinous. Sometimes there is poetry.

Dreams escape us as we cross over to the
Latter half of the final month of a year so
Strewn with carnage. "Are you seeing this too? Tell me."

At times the creativity coils slow like the
Python. I prefer to just gently tug the whiskers
Of a napping jaguar and see what happens.

James, the "D" stone has no color, lost in light.
There is no perfect diamond, poem or year.
With the deftness of a dream a great beginning comes.

...*beyond the worst.*

I cannot smell your perfume—alas, is that jasmine and lemongrass?
A start fraught with disaster—a poisoned evening?
Sit with me a moment, things might get worse.

I cannot taste your wine—alas, the pinot goes so well with the fish.
Now the meal is ruined too. The poison is real.
Sit with me a moment, things might get worse.

I cannot hear your praise—alas, what did you call me?
This conversation is the poison's new victim.
Sit with me a moment, things will get worse.

I cannot see your face—alas, is there an approving smile?
This poison is taking effect much too quickly.
Sit with me a moment, things will get worse.

I cannot feel your lips—alas, was that a kiss?
There is no antidote and the poison spreads.
Sit with me a moment, things will get worse.

The last traces of poison are gone. Moment
To moment I sit here at your oak casket, Jim.
In the Beloved's embrace we pass beyond the worst.

...brought you here.

So, where to start? This is not the beginning.
Sweet amnesia, somehow I have forgotten the way back.
No matter, in this sacred space, we are here.

There and again the habits of old intrude
On your progress. You have to press on and you have
The right to face your accusers, now call them here.

Living in this dream, I cannot help but think that
The rules of the game will change. This is way beyond
A faith in miracles. How is it I am still here?

Your hands alone craft a sacred gift. The paper
Needs to be clean & crisp, the folds straight & true.
You have to endure the moment, you have to be here.

Silence is best when the winds of fate come howling.
Tonight, compassion without any conversation.
The knock at the door—her eyes whisper, "I'm not here."

So, where to end? No, this is not the finale.
Despite the bitter remembering Jim, I will
Never forget the sacred words that brought you here.

... *Carcosa returns.*

No clouds, the lidless eyes of twin suns scorch my soul.
I turn from the dawn, the dark seas glimmer and beckon.
The longing for ancient Carcosa returns.

Poetry reading at The Court of The Yellow King.
Never say no to any lover of your work.
My tear-filled grief for Carcosa returns.

We want the unseen demons beneath the surface.
The crushing depths felt in every cold embrace.
Her desire for the ways of Carcosa returns.

Black stars rise and strange moons cross.
Sparkling cava pours and dark duels erupt.
The vengeance of lost Carcosa returns.

Silent cyphers screaming, the blood days are here.
Tatters of freedom remain and still rein.
James, do not pray that strange Carcosa returns.

Poisons are potent reminders of trespasses.
Any and all antidotes simply delay your death.
Now the ancient curse on Carcosa returns.

…come together.

Caustics are of no use against the alchemical
Torments of ones own making. Beneath the grimore's
Marbled endpapers a formula appears.

The keyboard clack clicks as I tap out the hack of
My own consciousness. I review the code and
Imagine the bytes beneath and the lost pointers.

Istanbul artisans know the gel-git tracing's
Beneath heaven's illness. Despite the design,
Worms feed—even on lost feathers of angel wings.

A desire beneath insane digests the lining
Of what I thought was my inner strength. My hidden
Disposition twisting, uncoiled and unpleasant.

Miss G. says, "The place you should go is Tangier.
Alice and I've spent three summers there, and it's fine."
The demons in the desert were beneath mentioning.

Morocco was already whispering promises in
My ear, the cool burn of claws beneath my scalp.
Sips of whiskey as poem and plan come together.

…*compel us.*

Everyday extraordinary—today you woke.
Elsewhere, yet another dead poet is counted.
These crisscross days, they sip and slice in crazy ways.

What is all this poetry? A salve to explore
Image and feeling or a bit of peppermint
Poorly wrapped and stale in the lingerie drawer?

Her madness invited an endearing sense of dread.
There are many trap doors that save and succor us.
Can your careful dance steps contain this despair?

The partial results of numerous failed
Experiments. I suppose it is a grave error to confuse
The Books of The Dead: Tibetan, Egyptian, Celtic.

I remember the wolves there in the London Zoo.
We shared some delicious words and succulent snacks.
Later, we were howling and the crowds were screaming.

The waltz intended and a trip extended.
She falls, never lands, floating in ecstasy.
When love pales, the hungers of poetry compel us.

…could escape.

A friend said my poem was haunted. I believed
In ghosts, so it seemed a possibility.
The poem corrected, "She said, "haunting," not "haunted.""

Hoping the buds survive the unexpected chill,
I imagine your pink cherry tree in bloom.
Later, sour unripe cherries crushed in ice coffee.

The Cailleach tells me that my love of olives for
Breakfast is related to my night in the Garden
Of Gethsemane. What did you dream for breakfast?

We confuse the meanings, mistaking silence for
Rejection. We worry, regretting the sacrifice
And yet our gifts are real, accepted and cherished.

There are too many dreams screaming in my head.
Behind my eyes the knives are drawn. A haloed moon
Drips red. I have to focus or be sliced to shreds.

So James, you have glimpsed the unspeakable abyss.
The white threads of anger were felted so thick,
So densely, none of your enlightenment could escape.

...*dream form.*

Question: Is a poem a container or contents?
I know I'm mostly water yet I can't flow
Easily from this shattered sake bottle.

Question: Are my metaphors too self serving?
The smoke clears, the spill dries, forgotten forest prayers
Offer a lost soulfulness. The door slides closed.

In your silence I held the dreaming. The writing
Guides the way. A lattice of longing so fragile,
I worry about selecting the next question.

So tiny, the Soul's etching on a shard of glass.
As I read the poem I do not notice the
Sharp cuts, the fingers' red tears. No more questions.

Answers, invisible like the air we breathe.
Fear fades, blinded by the realities exposed in
A soft reflection of shattered lead crystal.

It is 2AM Jim. Any hour is right and true
To toast the friendship that can melt the cullet and
Take the glassblower's soft breath, giving the dream form.

...every touch.

There are depths of feeling where the pressure will crush
The bones of our weaker selves. Soul divers know the
Dark, wicked dark, waters there. My turn. My time.

What are you buying today? Spirit does not accept
Cash or credit. Here we barter in belief, breathe
And blood—what else? Yeats says: "... was blessed and could bless."

Miss Frida puts three dead roses in her hair.
What could be more fitting fashion for my funeral?
Miss Paula smiles, the caretaker trimmed my eyebrows.

They tell you, we are here, these are the end times.
Yeh, you've heard that before. What are they selling?
Me, I am always late for those little armageddons.

Can these watercolor emotions resist this grief?
Beauty sustains us, yes, and the Mystery.
We can live through everything entwined in these briers.

So which is more greedy, to write about a friend's
Death or your own? Jim, dwelling in that mortal certainty
Moves the poetic imagination to cherish every touch.

...*everything.*

What is there to tell? Seeing through the veils to the
Other world—indescribable, best forgotten.
I confess to you, I do not know everything.

These fragile realities separated by
Seemingly impenetrable membranes of
Multiplicity. How do you describe everything?

Friends and acquaintances and unmentionables
Strolling the streets of London. In one night, to
Touch, to sight, to sample, to scratch—everything.

Séance—the ghost seated to my left has a message
For you. "Take off your mask." Eternal recurrence,
And yet again, everything repeats, everything.

So many unfinished things calling to us.
Turmoil in the imagination and the heart bleeds.
Even the poet cannot capture everything.

James K., you told the sidhe wolf that you were learning
To burn differently. In faery light you will be
Faced with a new darkness in everything.

...few endure.

This darkness is sticky, more like napalm than grease.
I am lost burning beyond a soothing coolness.
The question saves me, how much more can I endure?

They circle, high, out of sight, but your scent is an
Easy trail. We need these vultures of conscience
To pick clean our hypocrisy. Some pieces endure.

We debate the Spiral—its meaning in crash space.
The crypto-key dissolves in the bright discussion.
Rest assured my Friend, everything will not endure.

The mailbox is full of the stings of scorpions.
There is not enough time to plan anything.
The future ruined your reunion, yet you endure.

Help us James, aren't you the brother of Jesus?
The promised ending never comes. Please, tell me how
Many more second comings do we have to endure?

See this geomancy traced in the desert sand?
You know the spelling of words that are not spoken.
Poets share an understanding that few endure.

...focus there.

Have you traced the lines in your lover's right hand?
The future is there, time to savor the details.
Now look next to the iris of each eye, stare deep.

Have you traced the streaking comet in the night sky?
The day job exhaustions drag you to sleep too early.
The wonders of the world are not nine to five.

Have you traced the tears on a refugee's face?
Jesus sees the unreported atrocities there.
We are hollow witnesses to horrors and beauty.

Have you traced the panic piling softly around us?
The streets empty, empty of kindness, except
The plastic strands of color: purple, green and gold.

Have you traced the lies that swirl the storms of chaos?
The walls shudder and shake. The screams—your precious
Collection of poisons fall from the shelf and shatter.

Have you traced the Soul in the dreams of your Friends?
Ignore the trafficking of swipes and clicks and views.
Listen when I tell you James K., you must focus there.

...forever lost.

A noisy bar, nowhere special, just Tangiers.
In the far booth is Paul Bowles, the expat novelist.
You've recently arrived from Paris, never lost.

We really do not know how to count down the days.
Endless, forever, rise, set, none are for us.
Eternity to cross infinity—I'm still lost.

I trace the moonlight across the desires of touching
Your naked skin. I am awake, but this is your dream.
The Moon interrupts and asks, "Are you lost?"

Are you lost? An important and curious question.
Is there poetry here? Another query?
Can we please go back to when the answers were lost?

The pause is essential, then the venomous strike.
Bowles sits in the corner, arabesque tile suites the room.
The hand is near the mouth, the chance is not lost.

The desert—a baptism of solitude yet
No sheltering sky, only the Beloved's Eyes
And in that vision, I am holy, forever lost.

...*future awaits.*

Short of a horrifying miracle, she was
Frugal with her criticism as if we were
Sipping scorpion venom and not absinthe straight.

And the diagnosis: the heat beats true but too fast.
The odds of spontaneous combustion increase.
I look past the misfired round in the 45.

I know Vallejo worried this morning coffee
Was meant for someone else. When is a blessing
A missed chance of thievery? I need a refill.

You are here now, this is not counterfeit currency.
You are the paint bomb flash blast of pigments that
Even the most ardent phantom cannot evade.

Evidence of blood sport left on the bathroom wall.
The moscito lingered too long after enjoying
The off season buffet. Deadly tastes abound.

James, the path to immolation is not hastened
By a wonderful whirlwind. The burning is slow
And complete. A fabulous future awaits.

…heal us.

Our beloved Ophelia was buried today.
I was not there. Too many rats behind curtains.
Too many steak knives at the table—no breath.

Elsewhere we lost two more in a side of senseless
Violence. If these tears of grief were mindlessly
Collected I know I would drown. Please take these gifts.

Salt-water sorrows spiral with a symmetry
That provides no traction, like that black ice that sends
Us sliding through the guardrail and over the cliff.

I was already in freefall before that Thursday
Night. Now watch, all Acadie turns toward a friend,
Toward a neighbor, and yes, even toward a stranger.

We survived storms and wars and shooting and even
The panic and spurts of a broken blood feather.
Stained pages of memory cannot be cleaned.

Despite our blessings, you know that nothing is ever
The same. And please do not ask, "James, are you OK?"
Sadness and grief are not poisons—they heal us.

...*hidden doorways.*

The eyes close, the palms touch, the knees kiss the dirt.
Or a column centers a spinning disciple.
The Divine knows the Heart and the many ways to pray.

I have swept the path all week; all you need is a
Straw broom and the dance steps of Divine devotion.
These gathering blessings mingled among the dust.

Do you know these aggressions and transgressions,
Those above and beyond the usual forgiveness?
I cannot speak for the Divine, here or ever.

The Divine, behind the eyes of the One you Love.
Keep staring, keep dreaming. Not greed or desire,
Rather visions, made real over and over again.

Sweet Divine, never let me go. I am a twisted
Tight tourniquet in your hands, soaked, stained,
Yet sustaining. Each beat, disaster averted.

There are many paths that lead to the Divine.
James, you never ask about the Kingdom Within.
The secret silent keys that unlock hidden doorways.

...in sorrows.

The foyer is haunted by the soft scent of a
Decaying gecko. Some explorers never
Return. We merge and mingle incomplete sorrows.

On a lazy Sunday there is always more
Poetry to be written. The tour of a friend's
Rose garden is postponed. I sip slow sorrows.

Tomorrow, another classmate's obituary
Will be printed. Wait, some days this is not so.
Someday this will never be so. Sip more sorrows.

The lockbox is perfumed; the claw is small and
Covered in soft fur. My desires hopelessly
Inseparable from her sweet gifts and sorrows.

Hardware store aisle end cap reminds me that October
Still falls within the Season of Named Storms.
Clouds gather and spiral around other sorrows.

Not home, but wandering the streets of Tangier,
French radio beckons from the corner café.
No dance steps but I am never lost in sorrows.

...into place.

Dark calla lilies want to see the brown deepening
Of your eyes. They wait for you in the studio.
Do we want the artist, the artist's best or the artist's best work?

I chased the red-haired beauty through the weaving
Columns. She was wearing the midnight sky, both
Luminous and obscure in the same fleeting glance.

Dreams once stitched together are being undone
Along the steps and shuffles of paired polite guests.
More mysteries to explore after the mending.

Did we ever get permission to chart the heavens?
And the trespass? It is true I cut myself shaving
With the dull crescent of the waning moon.

Jim, your Soul needs the shade of ancient forests
And not the melting caress of the car park asphalt.
Some of the blackness and depths you fear are inside.

Darkness? This is not the time for sleep. The ceilings
Are coated black by the weariness of others.
OK, let's finger-paint the stars back into place.

... is your poetry.

No one, nobody, no man—you need an escape.
A Cyclops of singular vision and appetite
Has promised to eat you last. Pour the wine.

The pain has passed but the terror still lingers.
You recall her fingers around your rag doll throat.
The unloving closeness where you saw her fangs.

A bottle of wine and a bottle of hot sauce.
So what is the missing ingredient to this
Personal poetic alchemy? I can't say.

Fall awake - There is a breath from the other world
That lifts your spirits to unknown heights above
The mundane doubts of the day-to-day drudgery.

The world of objects exists without your blessing.
I can't give you leave to pretend otherwise.
The world outside thought is heavier than you can lift.

We need the pretensions of the wine critic.
The quality of Furies, Harpies and Muses
Builds flavor—bouquet. James, this is your poetry.

…just float.

Flock flight skyward, wing beats whirl and the spiral
Forms in your field of vision. What you see is real.
Never, never, doubt your sovereign experience.

I'm so sorry, there is no way back to before.
There is no pass go to tomorrow, either.
More broken promises, I slept through the night Lord.

Recurring dream: Another coffee date with
Nietzsche's Demon. She tells me she has given up
Drinking spirits for Lent. And I say "not again?"

Stray dog days wander the olive groves. No wonder
The week folds forward, Thursday trades with Tuesday.
I have stopped counting the lost, the days and the fingers.

We starve for advice to adore the fragments
Of our lives. Meanwhile others torture and crucify
Our story, to slake purposes hidden beneath.

You can't see the beauty in Saturn devouring
His children. Echoes of trauma—hungers reborn.
It's Quixotic quicksand James, don't struggle, just float.

…linger.

Midnight. The end has come, until next we meet.
The unreality dismantles as arranged.
Alas, no traces, only the memories linger.

Andalusian soundscapes with a simple click.
Federico, you're my best friend ghost poet but
We were never lovers, yet the rumors linger.

Betwixt and between—this is not on any map.
I close my eyes to the digital distractions,
The beauty of your mystery must still linger.

A Monday maelstrom is cleared by a mudslide of grief.
Choked in the sweetness of this spiral dream where
I hear those words: "do you have to let it linger?"

Welcome to the first ghazal of Two Oh One Eight.
James, you might be my favorite poet but
Forgetfulness asks politely, please do not linger.

You shoot the arrow directly into the blinding
Noonday sun. There are moments when timeless words
Are not welcome and my silent curses linger.

. . . meet you there.

There is a stitch; golden threads dance though the fabric.
Loops and knots closing so many open wounds.
Much of the healing is done elsewhere, not just there.

There is a snitch; one who betrays your darkest secret.
Despite all your precautions and security
The imprisoned soul finds a way out of there.

There is a twitch; the smallest of impairments,
In the eye, in the little finger. Cyphers that
The demise of the ego has begun there.

There is a switch; a shift, when you no longer use
The world's tragedies to prove you're right. You embrace
Compassion and love your enemy. Are you there?

There is a glitch; code hacked long ago, bits and bytes,
Copied and pirated. On to the reboot, restore,
Upgrade and patch. The work never seems done there.

There is a witch; beautiful in her obscure
Obsessions. She once told you J. K.: "The future
Is a strange and wonderful place." We will meet you there.

...more recollection.

I am ever becoming a thing of more knowing
And more unknowing. The spiral unrelenting,
Cuts in both directions, inward and outward.

Perhaps our lives are half dream and half nightmare
Yet we do not know which is which. Running headlong
Into terror instead of just falling into joy.

A desperate guilty war criminal drinks poison
At sentencing. Certainly, a form of justice
More humane than an impromptu firing squad.

Careless tending of the soul—the roots and the branches
Interleave, everything becomes inseparable.
Careful tending of the soul—ah, same results.

We all know those connect-the-dots puzzle books.
By your hand, the angel you pencil in, is a demon in my eyes.
This is how abject malice becomes public policy.

Where do our shadows go when we step in darkness?
Tell me James, I know you have done this a few times.
So for you, poetry is not escape, instead more recollection.

... move forward.

Delerium forced me overboard and
Jonah's whale saved me. Before that I was trapped
Between the strata of personal laments. It's natural.

Where is this Dream? The trust is lost. I cannot close
My eyes. And who can claim to know the trends as we
Shuffle tyrants for personal expression.

I called Hemingway a complex son of a –
She politely added, well aren't most artists?
A personal opinion of others is a good mirror.

I meet the eye of this great whale. The look of
Personal recognition surprises us.
The Silver Bank waters are calm and clear. I am both.

Thrashing about, digging for personal treasure?
We are already buried alive. Shift to a
Soft, subtle rise to the surface, float in quicksand.

We were once the same Jim. Falling, Rising, Living.
Each succession the Soul Trail becomes clearer.
Do not let the personal hold you back, move forward.

...*my light.*

Morning mist—I see the fading prayer flags draped
On the fig tree. What was it that I wanted from the future:
A smile, a kind word or a knife to cut these bonds?

What is hidden in the fog that lasts through lunchtime?
So many unsatisfied appetites linger
Into the future. The Unseen's table set before us.

I will not argue over the foretold malicious
Gestures of the one hand but do not trust and
Turn away from that poison blade in the other.

The beach is strewn with empty glass bottles, no messages.
Do you believe this wandering is penance
For some forgotten trespass? Rest and wait for dark.

When you look back, please see me when I held you in
My arms and not when I wheeled away hurtful
And weak. Hope embraces your forgiveness tonight.

Jim, the moon grants us a soft lunacy. I am
Stretched thin, to translucency. Soon I will be
Invisible—you will see my darkness and my light.

...my name.

How is it all year I have not seen your clear eyes?
Without such sights of wisdom and compassion
I am a turned ankle in the rushing madness.

We met a dozen years ago in October.
I was a poet wandering the thin places.
The world had already changed the month before.

In a hidden dimension you will encounter
The "Blue Shift." I am snared in the physics,
Reading your twelve poems, this last day of November.

Emotions swing from gratitude to frustration.
I curse and bless this Mystery spiraling
Around us. The wind has stripped the braches bear.

She holds you softly, leads you through the veiled
Door in the hillside. I look away, up into
The shining night sky and say your name: "Moon Pointer."

Jim, I taught you that the Eagle is not the King
Of The Birds. Under His wings scan and decipher those
Dark feathers. Today you will come to my name.

...my sanctuary.

"Sanctuary in Night, Mystery & Light..."
I wonder if this can ever be true for someone.
I have to believe words are some sanctuary.

The bell tower sounds an alarm as the waters
Spill, overflowing from your two cupped hands.
 They say raindrops and teardrops seek sanctuary.

I can be silent with you Love. The energies
Dance between us, even when we are not in sight
Of each other. Stillness—Soft—Souls—Sanctuary.

The poet closes his eyes and listens intently.
What did you tell me Salvatore, was it darkness?
No, Night is the poet's sanctuary.

What half is wasted? No one knows. I will tell you
This Jim, among the greediness for money,
For things and for people, there is no sanctuary.

I have left the stone walls and the iron fences.
I have left the glowing screen and the qwerty keys.
The wind, the trees, the sun are my sanctuary.

...*my steps*

So much sadness pours over me and now this body
Is broken. Some pieces of my Soul left years ago
And the spaces filled with greed instead of yearning.

Fountain pen ink is no match for the rain.
"I can never see you again." The writing flees
In illegible smears. The train is leaving the station.

How does this end, this grief? Tiny—Deep—These hidden
Punctures sometimes do not bleed at all, even
Those to the Heart, but always the suffering.

Hiraeth? Are those the words of longing that flood this
Modern complacency? Grief leads us to touch madness,
Then art. Then the road splits: more art or more madness?

These wounded missteps in this meandering
Mystery lead to trailblazing for others but
They cannot bring you Home. Follow your yearning Heart.

Something has happened, help me remember.
Jim, Beginning no longer has any meaning.
I have lost my way, even retracing my steps.

. . . my terrors.

And what about now? There is no beginning
To this poem. My mind rearranges the color
Of the days and I see greys instead of pinks.

I have wasted another day checking the
Accuracy of silence. I cannot answer
To the unconscious trespasses that occurred.

Broad patches of color, overlapping, stacked
And repainted. A massive softness that crushes
Many notions of landscape, still life or portrait.

Perhaps my dreaming and my waking will mix in
Some dance. Gesture and phrase, guide and praise; links break
And form in all directions, an everlasting chain.

Flames abound and forests bare, J. K., we never
Tire of your tale about meeting Blake's Tiger
And the asymmetry that saved your poetic eye.

A glance skyward, the dead tree gives so little shade.
The bright sun promotes the tears of our grief. Tonight,
The funeral pyre will warm us through my terrors.

...my things.

Ancient declarations are still relevant.
Tyranny finds the words of Adams, Franklin and
Jefferson less that a delight. Some know such things.

I am not carrion. My sky burial is a
Welcome event for the winged demons to
Sweep down and pick away at the tender things.

What die roll will save us? The campaign seems at an end.
I am trapped at the crux of the matter.
I scream her name: "Eleven" and wait for stranger things.

We flip upside down and foreclose on flim-flam-ville.
A billion-dollar valuation in the cypher
Of a drop of blood. Extinction brings new things.

The desert sand, cold like snow with no wetness.
A cloud ruined sunrise. Other blessings, no witness.
And the just retaking of Mosul—atrocities are not things.

Of course! Despite the remains, the moustache perfect.
Do not carry around last month's poem and
Please, oh please, James, stop touching my things.

...never miss.

Nostalgic reflection often as sensuous
As lipstick kisses on steam coated mirror glass.
Look at me, please just confess, what else do you miss?

Gents often blame the equipment. The rifling
Makes the bullet spin on target. They would not call
Her a marksman but that Annie, she did not miss.

A strange attractor, alone in the coffee shop.
The phase space is complicated to navigate.
At the table—"tell me, is it Mrs. or Miss?"

The grand uncertainty of slash, burn, splash and whirl.
We all failed Keats and lament the trip to Rome.
All flow to the opposite, some things are hit or miss.

Is there any advice that might have helped?
Here is something they often leave out. When you are
On the right path, the wall is impossible to miss.

Are we playing Three Card Monte James? So who is
The mark: the reader, the poem or the poet?
Just use the bent corner—that is a trick I never miss.

…no hazard.

Al Zahr was my friend and an old geomancer
Who preferred casting lots to lines in the sand.
The signs, seen or unseen, you must face your hazard.

Unresolved to this day, Edison and Tesla
Debated the nature of electrons, yet agreed
That poetry was a dangerous hazard.

Nib, ink and parchment help conspire sweet revenge.
Each course, as sumptuous as the invitation.
Then the last: death or desert. Which will you hazard?

A long challenging round of billiards ends.
Hours of well chalked cues and striking precision.
A lightning clean carom was the winning hazard.

I am finding the wonders and terrors of living.
Certain doubts fill an uncertain reality.
Raise your glass, a toast to blessing and hazard.

Despite our horror, each new year feeds the juggernaut.
The gemstones of the Soul pass undigested.
James, keep gathering these jewels, there is no hazard.

...Not at an End.

No worries, I am here with you in this darkness.
Open your eyes and see what I see in the brightness
Of your own heart. Vision spirals anew and beyond.

Illusions abound, veils and curtains shift unseen.
Some dreams melt away; others sift in a soft breeze
Or in the whisper of a lover. Moonlight helps.

The Tyger and The Beloved know the horrors
Are asymmetric. Yet the answers to most
Of the rhyming questions the poet asks are still "yes."

Did you see the Moon tonight? What if the answer
Is "no"? What if the answer is "no, never"?
You really are lost, aren't you? Not sure what else to say.

You realize too late her eyes are two arsenic
Mirrors. Chemistry confuses alchemy and
Death confuses Love. There is that moment James.

The night is dark, an air painted pinot noir.
The wine glass is empty, so few drops of kindness.
Two Oh One Seven? No, the world is Not at an End.

...not that poem.

The calendar says today is the last of August.
I 've already moved into September.
I 'm trying to catchup, stealing from the past.

Writing one poem a month, is that contagious?
Perhaps, but my poetry is self-inflicted,
And you know, Miss Stein says to always tell the truth.

Those gone and lost gods have left their claw marks on the
Old parts of my soul. The wounds are healed, stronger
In some places. The Night Guard patrol the darkness.

Torture is incomplete murder, not unlicensed sport.
Your rendition tapes destroyed but everyone
Is surprised how long the truth can hold its breath.

Crinkled mylar does little to chill the terror.
The chain link fences cannot contain freedom's cries.
We are all layers upon layers of anguish.

Somewhere is that poem you are searching for.
Today is much more desperate than other days.
James, I will tell you right now, this is not that poem.

...nothing else.

The label read "ELIXIR"—in an all caps font.
The bottle was ink—blue-black—now those sweet worlds of
Night and Darkness, could be captured on parchment.

September, tell me, what is left to be crossed?
The trespass was unavoidable but bloodshed?
Darkness, I cannot claim the presentiments.

Are you still writing about darkness? With a splash
Of malt vinegar and a sprinkle of sea salt
This twenty-one cent kale is the best salad ever.

Your autumn light is poor at hiding my darkness.
The South is still warm for a cloak. Soft nightmares beacon,
Perhaps to borrow that old velvet mantle.

The impending balance of the equinox offers
Little comfort this year. We confuse so much.
The charge, the spin, yet we can survive the darkness.

There is the sinking—your whole form embraced by the
Dim waters, then the current takes you into darkness.
Are you writing? Living is an art like nothing else.

...of endarkenment.

Enlightenment, malignant in its damp blindness.
The water oak rots from the inside, out of view.
Somewhere a poem mentions my endarkenment.

Impossible things before breakfast? Try three key
Limes squeezed into a Japanese cold brew dark roast.
Taste, now you know what I mean by endarkenment.

On Thursdays, I despise my imagination.
Sometimes the week recovers. Savor the holy
Trinity of herbs and scents of endarkenment.

After supper, we talked all night in the olive grove.
The denials stretch centuries past the cock's crow.
Jesus taught me a lot about endarkenment.

James, you could lie and say that demon claws lead to
Your bleeding arm. No one believes a poor manicure
And nervous scratching leads to endarkenment.

The storms test our limits as failures fold around us.
The death of a school chum stretches our mortality.
Disenchantment comes with the lack of endarkenment.

... *of living.*

Gypsy cello—Spanish guitar—tonight deep art.
The Duende takes the floor and my gaze is always
Just a moment behind her razor sharp dance steps.

Closing time approaches. My Muse is washing
Glasses behind the bar. Sips of bitter, sour
Emotions sustain the silent conversation.

Who put my dreams on consignment? My Angel is
In the back cleaning up. There is the seeing and
The seen—the buying and the bought—it's a good night.

I know there is always darkness before the day.
We demand "light" everlasting to shine on our
Faces and deny the Shadow—to our peril.

The triskelion spins and cuts these knotted,
Superficial ties. Now I can fall faster in sweet
Acceptance. Do not worry, I am not alone.

On the most normal of mornings, be inspired.
Let the beauty flow through you, ignore the tears.
To touch the Soul is the fear and the art of living.

...of sovereignty.

The shift is subtle, the liquor clouds as the
Distilled herbs bloom in the presence of cool waters.
Slow sips contemplate the strong lingering tastes.

I suppose we fear that the annihilation
Will be incomplete. A fragment alone—even the
Best of me left behind, might feel abandoned.

Two months is not a long absence. The fondness
Remains but no desire for the precious
Excesses of our previous relationship.

I have heard said, "The desert is an ocean..."
So is that the mystery, the attraction?
Only swimmers on this cave ceiling, mark the lost waters.

A noetic archeologist has ardent
Regard for the creative spirit. Jim, there are
Always quiet letters lost in the mail.

Writing in darkness, the pen scratches out sharp
Desires at a distance. In the true dissolution
Of boundaries there is no loss of sovereignty.

...open seas.

Do we make our own monsters, or do they make us?
The claws and fangs, the mirrors and makeup.
We lose track of what is real and what is important.

I can't help you—I don't hide this broken wing.
I fell trying to save the world, I could not yet fly.
Now I just walk around town giving out feathers.

My cycles are off. I keep spelling circadian
As cicadian. No letter "r" and a big
Difference between the hours and the years.

Flailing? I am sure you can imagine that from
Some angle this motion might look productive.
You glance away to quiet the visions in your mind.

James, your destiny will always cross swords with who
You were. There are facts in your fiction and fiction in
Your facts. The duel always ends in someone's death.

"Thank you for your interest in our expeditions…"
The last time you were away I dreamed the desert sky.
Now I see a barque, full sail, carving the open seas.

...or night.

Each sip is precious, drinking from each other's grief.
Souls mingle then are torn apart but flames remain.
That fire is a gift. This will take most of the night.

Moonlight, silver crescent, sharp against my throat.
What pleas would grant me another day of writing?
This happens so often, yet I cannot fear the night.

The Beloved lifts Theresa from the floor.
Winds of passion, the cloak rustles, folds, flowing.
Here, feel this Divine Ecstasy, in the darkest night.

Sometimes the sunlight is more dangerous. A target
So well illuminated, any pause means the end.
Moving among such brilliant arrows I pray for night.

The final alchemy? This is far from over!
The ingredients, the proportions and the timing.
To see the stars, we need to wait until night.

Federico's Heart opened wide to embrace the Moon.
What else could any eyewitness account add?
Anyway Jim, I was not there, day or night.

...sea chantey.

Seeing things in black and white, you can rarely tell
That the blood spiraling down the drain is really
Just chocolate syrup—unless your own is spilled.

What is the safe distance from your darkest secrets?
Delight and sorrow—the fragrant rose and piercing thorns.
What are we to each other? Five paces, turn and fire.

The nib of the pen carves through the emotion,
Setting in place the envisionment. Cold water
Screams rarely provide any satisfying terror.

I reflected on the failed harvest and wonder
Over the defeat and the blame of liberty.
We do not see the blood seeping from the asphalt.

The dervish orbits the column and poetry flows.
This is an inertia that spins me through the
Fatigue that challenges the creative spirit.

There is a storming chorus that reminds you of your
Insignificance. James, I am so pleased to
Finally hear your own voice in this sea chantey.

...so drink.

The clocks turn back, but no hour of sadness is lost.
Jays screech and morn the oaks gone before the storms.
No restful shade, no escape, shallow breath, sunlight glare.

 Custom alloy wheels melt in the street, shimmering.
Modern metal cannot endure ancient grievances.
We are burning, send for a shaman or a poet!

I wake up. Now the cracks in the paint are bleeding.
Something is not working; I bought the wrong primer.
Another project gone malignant and awry.

Free falling—all night long—I think I love you.
You are Dead at what: 66, 64, 67?
Numbers beyond my father, maybe not me.

"Not at an End"—poetic words you once wrote James,
Before blasts and bullets ripped through quiet prayers.
As-Salaam-Alaikum—Wa-Alaikum-Salaam.

Whiplash of emotion, yet this is where we thrive.
Tears stream from sugar cane joy to rock salt sadness.
Absinthe green pales to the white of arsenic—so drink.

...*something else entirely.*

Sometimes I dream of floating, other times of flying.
Clouds just look fluffy, I can feel their sharp edges.
And lightning cuts you in places you don't know.

Sometimes I dream of floating, other times of walking.
I followed him off the boat and to the shore.
Sundown, fire on the beach and fresh fish with bread.

Sometimes I dream of floating, other times of diving.
Deep and eye to eye with the squid of my nightmares.
The flash of color and the tearing of flesh.

Sometimes I dream of floating, other times of dying.
The certain things in life are so comforting.
I woke this morning and I will sleep tonight.

Sometimes I dream of floating, other times of forgetting.
There is so much beauty here; the greedy soul
Wants it all. Appetite or addiction and the difference?

Sometimes I dream of floating, never of poetry.
James, my eyes are wide open as you turn the
Desert mirage into something else entirely.

... Tell me.

Tell me, are you transparent or invisible?
Do you prefer being exposed or hidden?
Is this silence a question or the answer?

Don't tell me about the uneasiness that wakes
You at half past midnight. Now, even this fruitless
Fatigue cannot move us toward the rest we need.

I can't tell if the storm is adding to the
Turmoil I feel. Rain and wind beaten souls are silent.
I am waiting for the truth to be exposed.

Please tell me, what fire drives your sacred reduction?
A thickening sweetness—a savoring, not meant
For strangers. I don't want to taste, I want the fuel.

No, they can't tell, tragedy or comedy?
We are all too much of mostly the wrong things.
Inauthentic and fabricated, often well written.

Tell me James K., these poems, are they sketches
Of the soul—shadows, signposts, silhouettes?
Do I have to ask this again and again? Tell me.

...the challenge.

Is life toil in alternating darkness and
Fluorescence? I would be interested in saving
Daylight if we did not also destroy the night.

I dreamt that my arrogance burned in the fires of
A distant star and my soul bathed in that light.
More heat than illumination was the complaint.

The white gesso flows thick over the abstract
Adventure. Attempts at form and folly, color
And catastrophe. These choices create a painting.

Demons of unknown monikers hide within all
Your qwerty blurts and auto correct missteps.
A digital thread of grave disregard and trespass.

So many tastes forgotten. Memories avalanche
The emotions of a bland and blended life.
Come bury me in those spiced times, seasonings past.

Move past a morning of fear and projections.
Call the crew to climb the masts, our sails can catch new winds.
Always, James, the change drives the change, meets the challenge.

...the hanging tree.

I want your sugar raw, unrefined, and
Unrestricted. Tracing the edges of your
Dark crystalline desire, ever so slow to dissolve.

The calendar grid already slices the flesh
Of the first month into neat squares of misery.
The countless drops of blood are held from view.

I knew your praise last year was off key and maybe
A little sour. These things do not bother me,
I drink malt vinegar straight from the bottle.

I am windproof, the flame from my father's favorite
Lighter. Perhaps a mistaken metaphor,
Sentimental smell of the flint strike and lighter fluid.

James, I can't answer to the horrors of the world
Or even my failures on this first week of the
New Year. So please, stop pressing the replay button.

The future is full of roofing nails resting in the grass.
Lush steel and green blades, both cold on bare soles.
I prefer the dry, brown dust, beneath the hanging tree.

...the mirrors.

We practice the ways apart and the ways together.
Have we found the reverence and gratitude there?
The rough edges sooth to a new imperfect gift.

Fingertips scented with fresh rosemary, wrapped
The fine china teacup. Lavender eye shadow,
Matching ascot—she was taken seriously.

You should be held by eyes that are already
Rich with seeing. Avoid those greedy glances,
Leering and hungry. Some artists steal, the wrong things.

I carefully watched the knife as she shared
A slice of her cake but I wanted to taste her
Madness, the dark flames, the fertile realms of her soul.

There is a lost reflection, a moment of
Brilliance purloined by faux shiny things.
Altered intensions in some other reality.

Jim, let's stay together here, apart from false desire.
Holy waters of a hot bath; the steam praises
The heavens and dismisses all the mirrors.

...the modern.

A banquet of close friends, strangers, enemies
And some pieces of me. All feeding, yet still ever
Hungry for the quick passing of the months ahead.

There was the Twelfth Night of 1897.
I survived, others attending did not.
The story is unfinished, part one at an end.

Aware, unforgettably aware, moist at the
Surface of the corpse cold aluminum bottle
Of beach wood aged brew. Tell me, where is the King?

How else do we sustain the ancient virtues?
The blood days are here. Never heard of virtue or blood?
You know we have much work to do, the time is now.

James, I would not encourage such attitudes.
Poisons are potent potions of past remembrances.
Not every antidote is wrapped salvation.

The suppression of our natures continues.
We are the true monsters who abduct our false selves
From the deep dark nightmare slumbers of the modern.

...the next frost.

The wave approaches, now filling half the sky.
There was never a time you could turn and escape.
Tears from a thousand years of joy bring sweet destruction.

Bodies pressed close, overflowing grasps of flesh.
Only when you close your eyes and at just the right
Moment, you can see the light around the body.

Her fifty-inch flat screen met her sledgehammer.
A daily nature augury brings her news of the universe.
Oh, and on game day just bring her to my place.

The silence in the snowy fields cannot hold
A candle to the desert night. Dune spirits are
Fast and quiet, they know the whispers of love and death.

Jim, I saw you talking into the ear of the
Donkey that morning Jesus rode by. I can't
Recall, was this in Jerusalem or in Fes?

A fire burns, warming the room. The man in the black
Coat turns, sits and gives the Blessing. Outside the
Bitter forgotten cold makes plans for the next frost.

...the stabbing.

The last domino falls, the workweek is done,
For now. I cannot recount the insignificant
Accomplishments—The best, the worst, you know the crimes.

There is a lot of talk about "The Other."
Some foreign dignitary of inferior rank.
All this attention, so tell me, are you to blame?

You know, your sovereignty depends on no one.
That is the idea. Do not call me to supper
Expecting me to prepare the meal. I am the One.

You know the phrase: "Ain't no one like me but me."
Torn apart, put back together, over and over.
We are this perfection and we did ask for this.

Break with the chains of tradition that enslave us.
I know the fear, the threats, the wounds, the soul's emergence.
Sit with me, I will call the healers to come.

James, there is an aloneness that can break the camel's back.
The desert sand makes for a soft sweet landing.
Ah, then the knives come out, ready for the stabbing.

...these days?

I feel the grief of lost days and trampled dreams.
Doomed wisdom is sinking the Solomon Islands.
Flat world, round world, the twisting blade is never good.

These are thirst-stricken times when cobras beg for
Water from strangers. Are your outstretched arms the
Cool embrace of baptism or fangs of vengeance?

Some confuse shell game profiteering for leadership.
Now we all wear white helmets and sift through
The bombed-out residences where truth once lived.

Knives stabbing the looking glass and another
Oligarch dead on the sidewalk. We count the pieces of
Silver again, certain now we have been cheated.

Dark writings are my forte' or some like to think so.
Do I want such extreme imaginings or
Terrible visons to haunt my readers?—perhaps.

Shards of crystal are caught in between my teeth.
Bad timing for a month that is toasting poetry.
Tell me truly James, what are you drinking these days?

... *to give.*

There are lost found poems, there are found lost poems.
In the sorted differences, January slips through your fingers.
Fear grips a freshly sharpened pencil, begin again.

The claws and fangs of this New Year are showing.
Have you been stealing from my collection of crucifixion nails?
The neglect of routine mending has finally let in the cold.

Everyone seems to have forgotten the gifts
They opened on that blessed morning last year.
We demand salvation but bring no charity.

I have filled the cracks in the mirror with gold.
I am not sure I cut myself any less while shaving.
The scent of Moroccan Myrrh fills the bath.

This year, the King Cake madness has come too early.
Garish charades and crowded parades overrun
The common sense of prudence and compassion.

I am gathering the colored shards of shattered
Contemplations. James, don't tell me what you want
Or what you think. Tell me what you are going to give.

... to justice.

"We hold these truths to be self-evident..."—you know
The words. Still tyranny is insidious and
Ever present. Whims of abuse crisscross the world.

How often are we just sitting in the dark,
Trusting that the beams from the projector room show some
Shape of the Light? And others, are just asleep.

Did you notice her? Did you see them drag her away?
Was your afternoon at the movies ruined?
Oh, you spectators of History in the making.

I can imagine Miss Viola behind those
Iron bars and I am reminded of Thoreau
And of St John of the Cross. Her spirit ablaze.

For those ahead of their time, the present can be
Such a disappointing affair. We all stand on
Her courage and glimpse a future rich in freedom.

More than a half-century later, a free pardon
And an apology. We celebrate Liberty by
Retracing those miles on the long road to justice.

...together.

The feather's edge was blue, a burning flame blue,
The flame of the furnace burners, when the heat kicks on.
Can this Firebird carry me beyond this wasteland?

The hands come together at the heart. In these moments,
Please be sure to praise beauty before blessing.
No more grasping, no more holding, only the breath.

I am feeling the sideways glance of the hawk.
The pain returns, and we are open all night.
Tell me about all these connected dismemberments?

There is a turning that orbits the truth. Not the
Spin that offers a lens of distortion. Rather
A bearing that honors the many centers, here and there.

No tears, no sweet returns. The Blood Moon is dry tonight.
The exhaustion spreads, another failed attempt at
The impossible. What does all this really mean?

We are all corpses, not ready for the shroud,
The winding sheets or the oak box. The sun kept its
Promise, we too must rise, a new, a glow, together.

...too well.

Our hands are clasped—we say Grace around this table,
The work and wonder of our lives. For a moment
We forget the dreams that slip through our fingers.

Frankly I wondered at her breakfast order:
Two Faberge' Eggs, scrambled, with white cheddar.
The cook has his work cut out for him this morning.

Fine work at each place setting, crystal salt receivers
Hold white treasures that await the tamping of
Green onions. At meals we wonder at our worth.

Some advice: Do not demand to know the angel's
Work in this recent disaster. Let the critics
Wonder over the ashes as you take flight.

Time unravels us all so beautifully
Beyond the wonder and work of triumph and defeat.
A grain of wisdom among the piles of rubble.

Some words are sugar cubes, slotted spoons, green faery sips.
Jim, there is the work and there is the wonder.
When confused, the greedy soul drinks all too well.

…*uncanny shadows.*

Desperate times, I filled my pillow with the
Ashes of my failed scribbling from last month.
No inspiration, just more and more night terrors.

There was no comfort in his archived photos.
False hopes flourish in the rotting decay of guilt.
In anger, she deleted the laptop's hard drive.

A beautiful sight from shore, the storm layers
And builds. We forget the shipwreck of our lives,
Trapped in the delight of our own desolation.

Even the most beautiful eyes are not enough
To sustain any vision of the future.
Steamed milk frothiness, I kissed her lips again.

There is deep work that has to be done alone.
Candles burn all night as we rip out the threads
Of inappropriate stitching—a darkened poetry.

Do not worry, fear twists the in-between places of the
Imagination. So, like most mystics James,
Your inner light casts odd and uncanny shadows.

…was lonely.

The whirlwind was lonely. What was the explanation
For the attraction? At the swirling center
I could see the future breaking loose of the chains.

I threw fire into the whirlwind, spinning flames
And heat burning away the things I did not need.
What other elements could satisfy as fuel?

I kicked sand into the whirlwind, the motion
And grit polishing the rough edges I did not need.
What other failings could serve as payment?

I poured water into the whirlwind, the refreshing
Splashes washing away the fears I did not need.
What other talents could satisfy as a gift?

I whispered love poems into the whirlwind.
Then came a stripping of the words I did not need.
Now the Soul could hear my silent spiral song.

James, you know the truth. At the swirling center,
You could see the greying blur—shredded angel wings
And broken demon claws. The whirlwind was lonely.

...*wild patience.*

We are never the person they claim. Our rope is
Twisted tight. Some special knife work is in order.
There are strands here that do not belong.

Over coffee Vallejo elucidates how
In this hyper-wired-world, that the sorrows of
December and January bleed into March.

One day the river considers, no I will not
Cross that line. I will not flow to the ocean.
Do you know the floodwaters that you have caused?

I know you feel this in your chest, the air seems thin.
In the Other World there is a tightening tourniquet.
Yes, it is personal, we are being saved.

I will never forget that you asked me to
Write you a poem.   Maybe today that work will
Be finished. I still have some of your ashes.

The pecans are blooming Jim. Their flowers long for
Sun and rain and that special something that will move
Them on their path. Know truly this wild patience.

…with honey.

Where did I first meet him? In the drinking halls
Below street level, counting the forenoons and
Afternoons, full of whiskey notes and traded promises.

Beauty and Truth, these are mountainsides exposed
By the dawn sun but I have overslept and
My critical eye is blind to what I need to be shown.

The swarm: crawling layers of warm regret and
Swollen disappointment. What are the right weapons
In this wrong fight? A double-blind study of promise.

Now that you see the Truth behind the pasteboard mask
Can you really go back to that well-worn turn by turn?
The polished shield becomes the polished mirror.

These emotions scar a blank sheet in the notebook
Of some poet. Silent secret leers are stolen
Between glances of greed—afternoon turns to night.

Golden lichen faithful to the crumbing limestone.
Step carefully James, Beauty is underfoot in
All directions. This absinthe is sweetened with honey.

...*yes and go.*

Yes, I feel the unease, the speed increasing.
We are on a slingshot orbit and keep missing
The moment of release. Are you ready to go?

Yes, ignore the walking corpses and their many
Uninspired callings. I am tracing footprints
Left by your imagination.   Why did you go?

Yes, most times a poem is so easy to lose.
The shrieking surrounds us, yet a safer place alludes
The crowd. No one knows whether to stay or go.

Yes, I lost track of the days—a much needed retreat.
Bygone times? No, I do not miss their waspish
Affections. I am not sorry to see them go.

Yes, night flurries and the possession fails for now.
The long coat and the bowler hat assume their roles.
Soft tracks in the snow await, it is time to go.

Yes, last night while you slept the universe ended.
At dawn, you cannot count the many things reborn.
James, now there are just two things left, say yes and go.

...yes, silence.

For the fire, the burning is everything. The flames
Will never know the cotton's softness and the
Unspun fibers are blind to the flickering colors.

Warm curves among a thread count in the eighteen
Hundreds and yet somehow the naked softness
Of your dreams is the attraction. Poetry is real.

Kindness is not softness, rather the hammer
That nails you to The Cross. A salvation against
The answers to violence from all directions.

In secret, I crave the softness of your presence.
The effervescence of a fresh bottle of Brut
Opened before the party. Yes, diamonds are hard.

Much has happened before the sword is drawn.
Ore chiseled from the mine—the furnace reveals
The softness of the steel—the wheel its sharpness and shine.

James, sometimes a poem must end in softness.
There is the commiseration of words on a page,
Voices always ending in silence—yes, silence.

…your art.

Set aside your notions of the wild
And let the wind scatter your ashes.

Set apart your notions of the past
And let the seas dilute your acids.

Set asunder your notions of the guilty
And let the leaves bury your altars.

Set apart your notions of the modern
And let the sunlight dry your anguish.

Set aside your notions of the righteous
And let the fires burn your anger.

Set asunder your notions of the future
And let the mystery shape your art.

…your eyes.

I cannot quote the Latin, there is no escaping
The "tears in things." Yet I ponder and piddle
In the small spaces pretending safe in this storm.

The butterflies flee from his beard. I follow
Whitman as the colored wing beats led us to
Your unmarked grave. This was a trip that we had to make.

Thrown into the middle of things I draw patterns
In the sand. Everywhere a stranger, yet at ease.
A seer of all nightmares and of all dreams.

So this is the hand I am dealt, chasing
The phantom of my future self. Slices of
Reality shuffle in her well-manicured fingers.

Jim, you were not there when the ants, scorpions,
Birds and many unseen things took turns picking
Through their favorite delights. This was my passing.

The Inner and Outer and Other Worlds touch
The tears that flow from seeing the beautiful
Intersections of grief and joy. Open your eyes.

…your poetry.

The Atchafalaya is grey with a tint of rusted bronze.
The trees leafless, listen—something under the waters
Speaks to me on this February afternoon drive.

There is a tremor in my right eye, ever so slight.
A forgotten bio-programmed reminder,
Selected long ago for just this event.

Weekend parade aftermath—the streets are strewn
With stands of beads, the colors of power, justice
And faith abound. Landfill treasures of the future.

Bayou side. Not knowing the source, I hear a
Beautiful lament. Later the troubling news,
Ophelia was pulled from the waters the week before.

Icicles on the roofline, parades cancelled,
Mardi Gras is here. Mint leaves frozen ready
For the glass, if I can bear the unpleasant morning.

Purple, gold and green, you know the colors?
James, I remember the green rooftops in Marrakesh
And the tourist carrying a book of your poetry.

CPSIA information can be obtained
at www.ICGtesting.com
Printed in the USA
JSHW041303170421
13677JS00002B/135